D1709136

Ted Turner: televi   5030
Stefoff, Rebecca   B Tur

Sebastian Middle

TED TURNER

Television's Triumphant Tiger

TED TURNER

Television's
Triumphant
Tiger

Rebecca Stefoff

GEC GARRETT EDUCATIONAL CORPORATION

Cover: *Ted Turner.* (Alan Weiner/Gamma Liaison.)

Copyright © 1992 by Rebecca Stefoff

All rights reserved including the right of reproduction in whole or in part in any form without the prior written permission of the publisher. Published by Garrett Educational Corporation, 130 East 13th Street, P.O. Box 1588, Ada, Oklahoma 74820.

Manufactured in the United States of America

Edited and produced by Synthegraphics Corporation

Library of Congress Cataloging in Publication Data

Stefoff, Rebecca, 1951-
   Ted Turner, television's triumphant tiger / Rebecca Stefoff.
      p. cm. — (Wizards of business)
   Includes index.
   Summary: A biography of entrepreneur Ted Turner, who, after a number of diverse achievements, pioneered the world's first twenty-four hour, nonstop news station and changed the history of television.
   ISBN 1-56074-024-8
   1. Turner, Ted.   2. Businessmen—United States—Biography—Juvenile literature.   3. Sports team owners—United States—Biography—Juvenile literature.   4. Telecommunication—United States—Biography—Juvenile literature.   5. Seamen—United States—Biography—Juvenile literature.   [1. Turner, Ted.   2. Businessmen. 3. Television.]   I. Title.   II. Series.
HC102.5.T86S84   1991
384.55′5′092—dc20   91-32774
[B]   CIP
                                                                      AC

Contents

Chronology for **Ted Turner**

1938	Born on November 19 in Cincinnati, Ohio
1963	Took over family billboard business after father's death
1970	Bought Channel 17, an Atlanta television station
1976	Began broadcasting nationwide on WTBS; bought the Atlanta Braves baseball team
1977	Won the America's Cup sailing race with his yacht *Courageous;* became part-owner of the Atlanta Hawks basketball team
1980	CNN began broadcasting round-the-clock cable news
1982	Headline News began broadcasting
1986	Bought MGM Entertainment Company, a movie and television studio; sponsored the first Goodwill Games athletic event, held in Moscow
1988	TNT cable station began broadcasting
1990	Second Goodwill Games held in Seattle, Washington

Chapter 1

A Big Gamble

Sunday, June 1, 1980, was a very important day for Ted Turner. On that day, he changed the history of television.

Turner was a 41-year-old businessman in Atlanta, Georgia, who had invested $100 million in a brand-new television station. After many months of preparation, the station was scheduled to begin broadcasting at six o'clock that afternoon. It was called CNN, which stood for Cable Network News. As the name suggested, it was a **cable** station. (Terms in **boldface type** are defined in the Glossary at the back of this book.)

NEWS AROUND THE CLOCK

Cable television was still something new in 1980. At that time, only 15 million homes in the United States were wired to receive cable— about one household out of every five.

As the name also suggested, CNN was a news network. In fact, it was going to be the world's first 24-hour, nonstop news station. Nothing like it had ever been done before. It would carry only news around the clock, from around the world.

"I'm going to do news like the world has never seen news before," Turner boasted. "This will be the most significant achievement in the annals [history] of journalism."

Taking a Chance

Turner was so confident that CNN would be a success that he had gambled a huge amount of money on it. However, not everyone was so sure. Some people doubted that viewers would be interested in a full-time TV news station. But Turner pointed out that all-news radio stations were popular and successful, so why not all-news television?

Other people believed that the audience for cable TV was too small to keep an expensive operation like CNN in business. But Turner believed that cable TV had a big future. He already owned one very successful cable TV station, and he felt that cable would grow tremendously during the coming years, attracting new viewers every month.

Finally, a lot of people just didn't believe that an Atlanta businessman with a reputation for pulling crazy stunts could really challenge the three big broadcasting **networks:** NBC, ABC, and CBS. For years, these networks had been the country's only source of television news broadcasts. But there were those who claimed that if anyone could compete with the big networks on his own terms, it would be Ted Turner.

Ted Turner gambled his fortune on a cable news network—and changed the history of television. (©1991 David Burnett/Contact Press Images.)

A Colorful Figure

Turner was already a legend in the South, and he had become famous throughout the rest of the country as well. He was a colorful person who had strong opinions and liked to make them known.

Turner also had quite a reputation in the sports world. He was a famous **yachtsman,** the outspoken owner of a professional baseball team, the Atlanta Braves, and a part-owner of a professional basketball team, the Atlanta Hawks. Tall and handsome, he also had something of a reputation as a ladies' man.

A RISK-TAKING ENTREPRENEUR

But the thing that people found most interesting about Ted Turner was that he was an **entrepreneur,** a type of person who has always been greatly admired in American business. As an entrepreneur, Turner liked to think of himself as a pioneer, a leader in business rather than a follower.

But being an entrepreneur means being a risk-taker as well. Starting a cable news station was the perfect example of a new business venture that involved a big risk. If it did not succeed, Turner would have lost a large part of his fortune.

So, as the clock ticked on toward CNN's scheduled starting time, many people around the country and even around the world waited to see whether Ted Turner's big gamble would succeed or fail.

The Entrepreneur

An entrepreneur is someone who organizes and manages a business enterprise. The enterprise can involve a completely new product or service, such as Ted Turner's all-news cable TV station, or it can involve a product or service that is also offered by other businesses.

The most important qualities of the entrepreneur are that he or she enjoys challenges and is creative. An entrepreneur would rather lead than follow, and would rather be his or her own boss than work for someone else.

Ted Turner may go down in history as one of the greatest American entrepreneurs. In 1980, when he launched CNN, a business analyst named William Donnelly said of him: "If you look back at the people who have changed the American life-style, you find they're people like Ted Turner. His kind of energy, integrity [honesty], and willingness to take risks are very hard to come by. They're exactly what is missing today in America."

Chapter 2

The Countdown

The start-up of CNN was a race against time. Months earlier, Turner had announced to the world that the station would begin broadcasting at 6:00 P.M. on June 1. Since that time, everyone involved in CNN had been racing to get ready.

It seemed that there were a million things to do—and a million problems. One by one, most of the problems had been overcome. Now, just a few hours away from Zero Hour, CNN staff members waited nervously at the station's **bureaus** in New York City, Washington, D.C., Chicago, and San Francisco in the United States. There were also two overseas bureaus, in London, England, and Rome, Italy.

Staff members at the bureaus would be part of CNN's newscasts, providing nationwide and worldwide coverage of events. And Ted Turner was already talking about opening more bureaus—maybe even one in Beijing, China. First, however, CNN had to get off the ground.

LIVE NEWS

The whole point of CNN, as Turner had explained to the people he hired to work at the station, was to provide round-the-clock, live coverage of news events. This is what would make CNN different from the network news programs. The networks packaged the news into half-hour segments and broadcast these segments at certain set times of the day and night.

Only on very rare occasions did the networks interrupt their scheduled broadcasts of soap operas, game shows, and prime-time programs to cover news live—that is, to report on an event while it is happening. According to Turner, CNN's big advantage was that it would provide live coverage of the news. And instead of squeezing all the news into a thirty-minute package, CNN would be able to stay with each news story for as long as necessary for complete coverage.

Live news seemed like a wonderful idea, and the staff of CNN was looking forward to working on it. But in order for CNN to look good on its first day, the station needed some important news to broadcast. The month of May 1980 had been full of exciting news stories. For the past few days, however, there had not been much news of any great importance.

A Hot Story

One story did look promising, however. A few days earlier, a black man named Vernon Jordan had been shot while visiting the Midwest. Jordan was an important leader of America's civil-rights movement. Fortunately, he was not killed, and was taken to a hospital in Fort Wayne, Indiana, to recover.

Following the shooting, the White House had announced that the President of the United States, Jimmy Carter, would fly to

Fort Wayne from Washington, D.C., to visit Jordan on Sunday, June 1. This was to be CNN's first day. Live coverage of the President at the hospital would be a terrific story!

The CNN producers arranged for a camera to be placed outside Jordan's room, in the hallway of the hospital. The big networks were there, too. However, they were planning to record the President's visit and broadcast just a few seconds of it later, on their regular evening newscasts.

Only CNN was prepared to offer live coverage of the President at the hospital. This would be a great beginning for the station. It would show viewers the advantages of live news, and it would prove that CNN could compete with the networks.

A Difficult Problem

There was one difficulty, though, and it was a big one. CNN's coverage from Fort Wayne would be cut off at 6:30 P.M. exactly. This was because the station had already arranged for a news update on the Middle East to be sent from Jerusalem by satellite starting at that time.

Ordering the satellite transmission from Jerusalem had been very expensive, and if CNN cancelled it, the station would have to pay for it anyway. So the decision was made to broadcast the Jerusalem report as scheduled.

As a result, CNN had only thirty minutes to get a live story about the President and Vernon Jordan. That half-hour was between 6:00 P.M., when the station would start broadcasting, and 6:30 P.M., when the Jerusalem report would begin. However, there was no way to know when the President would arrive to visit Jordan, how long he would stay, or when he would leave. The odds were against his visit taking place during the necessary half-hour.

CNN, the first all-news television station, went on the air in 1980. The station was fortunate to get a major scoop in its first half-hour of broadcasting. (Mike Keza/NYT Pictures.)

On the Air

The mood was frantic inside the CNN newsroom. The **anchors,** David Walker and Lois Hart, sat behind their desk, waiting to say their first words.

With a few seconds to go, the anchors faced the camera. Viewers' screens were filled with shots of a satellite dish and of the newsroom. Then the anchors appeared, sitting at their desk, looking relaxed and confident. They spoke.

"Good evening. I'm David Walker."

"And I'm Lois Hart. Now here's the news."

Just like that, CNN was on the air.

The news team covered several stories. But all the while, in another part of the newsroom, several producers were hunched over the TV monitor that showed what was happening in the hospital hallway in Fort Wayne. They saw only a closed door.

The President had finally arrived at the hospital and had gone into Jordan's room sometime before six o'clock. He was in there now. Would he come out before 6:30? The tension mounted as the minutes ticked by. The door remained closed. "Come on out of there, Jimmy," one of the producers kept muttering under his breath.

Scoring a Victory

Hart and Walker introduced a story about a murderer, then an update on the eruption of Mount St. Helens in the state of Washington, then a feature on airline safety. At 6:21, the station began to broadcast its first commercials. But in the middle of the commercial break, the Fort Wayne monitor showed Jordan's door opening and the President coming out. He was ready to answer questions from the reporters in the hall.

"Forget the commercial!" shouted one of the producers. "Go live!"

So at 6:22, CNN did something that is hardly ever seen on the big-three networks. It interrupted a commercial for live news coverage. All at once CNN was broadcasting the President's press conference in the hospital *while* it was happening, before any of the other networks could show it. CNN had scored a big victory!

Producers and technicians in CNN's control room monitor cameras from around the world, checking for fast-breaking stories. (Alan S. Weiner/NYT Pictures.)

A New Fear

The President stood and answered questions about Jordan's condition and about civil rights. Suddenly, CNN's producers began to experience a new fear. What if the President kept talking right up past 6:30? They were scheduled to put on the Jerusalem report, and it was too late to change that arrangement now. But it would look awful if the station cut off the President right in the middle of an interview!

It was 6:29—less than a minute until the Fort Wayne connection would have to be cut off. The same producer who had been urging the President to come out of Jordan's room was now feverishly muttering, "Wrap it up, Jimmy, end it."

Almost as if he had heard the producer's plea, President Carter paused and then said, "Thank you very much," and walked away. The press conference was over. The clock showed 6:30. Right on schedule, the Fort Wayne picture faded and the screen showed a reporter in Jerusalem.

The newsroom exploded into cheers. "God has looked down on CNN," cried one producer, "and said He likes us!"

The world's first cable news station had met its first big challenge. It had gotten on the air on schedule, and it had handled an important story live. But it would be some time before Ted Turner knew whether his dream station could survive—whether his big gamble had paid off.

Chapter 3

Early Years

Ted Turner was born Robert Edward Turner, III, on November 19, 1938, in Cincinnati, Ohio. His parents had met and been married in Cincinnati, although his father, Robert Edward Turner, Jr., was originally from Sumner, Mississippi. Ted's only sibling was a younger sister, Mary Jane. She was also born in Cincinnati, when Ted was three years old.

A FATHER'S INFLUENCE

It is clear from his stories of his boyhood that his father was an extremely important influence in young Ted's life. Ed Turner, as Ted's father was called, was a strict disciplinarian who had a burning desire to be successful. During Ted's childhood, Ed Turner filled his son with that same desire to succeed.

Ed Turner was brought up on a Mississippi cotton farm.

During the **Great Depression** of the 1930s, many Americans were driven to poverty. Ed Turner's father—Ted's grandfather—was one of them. He lost everything he owned, including the farm.

Perhaps it was this tragic experience that made Ed Turner so desperate to succeed. Ted Turner recalls, "I came out of a Depression family, where my father started with absolutely nothing. He thought that the way to be successful was to make a lot of money and have a lot of riches and power."

Moving Around

Ed Turner had originally planned to take over the family farm. But now that the farm was gone, he moved to Cincinnati to make his own way in the world.

Ed started a billboard business. He sold advertising space on the large signs that were springing up along the highways, country roads, and city streets of the United States.

When Ted was nine years old, Ed Turner moved the family to Savannah, Georgia, because he felt that his business would be more successful there. This move was important, because it brought the Turners back into the South. So not only was Ted Turner the son of a Southerner from Mississippi, but he grew up in the South from the age of nine.

A Proud Southerner

Today, Ted Turner is proud of being a Southerner, and has always identified strongly with the traditions and history of the South. His favorite movie is *Gone with the Wind,* the epic story of Atlanta and the South during the Civil War.

One reason Ted was so determined to make his Atlanta-based television empire a success was that he resented the way that the television industry was controlled by people in the North, especially in New York City, where the big-three networks are based. He wanted to show that the South could compete with the North—and win.

SCHOOL DAYS

Not long after the Turners settled in Savannah, Ted's father enrolled him in the Georgia Military Academy, located just outside Atlanta. Ted was in the fifth grade. He did not have an easy start at the academy. He arrived at school six weeks after classes had begun, so he was already behind his classmates, with a lot of work to be done to catch up.

Ted felt he would have to be extra tough in order to prove himself to the other boys. So he quickly let it be known that he was not afraid to fight. He did get into some fights, and was proud that he never backed down.

Two years later, Ted started attending another military academy, the McCallie School, in Chattanooga, Tennessee. Here he tried out for a number of sports teams: football, basketball, and baseball. Unfortunately, he was not very good at any of them.

Discovering Sailing

However, Ted soon discovered another sport, one that he loved and continues to enjoy to this day. That sport was sailing. He entered many sailing events and races. Although he did not win many of them, he attracted a great deal of attention for his bravery and nerve.

Turner discovered the joy of sailing when he was a teenager, and he still loves the sport. He is considered one of the world's great yachtsmen. (Cunningham/Gamma Liaison.)

Ted always sailed as hard as he could and took chances. His bold, daring style of sailing earned him the nickname Capsize Kid, for the number of times his boats capsized, or turned over. He had another nickname as well: Terrible Ted, for his hot temper and his nervous, high-strung behavior.

FAMILY LIFE

Ted lived at military school from the fifth grade until high-school graduation, but he spent holidays and vacations at home. His relationship with his father probably played the biggest part in shaping his early years.

Ed Turner made it clear that he loved his son, but he was not always easy to get along with. He was very strict with Ted, and set high goals for the boy.

For example, Ted was supposed to read a book every two days. If he failed to do this, or to meet some other standard set by his father, he could receive a beating. Fortunately, Ted liked to read.

His favorite reading material was books about military heroes, such as Alexander the Great and Genghis Khan. He loved reading Greek and Roman myths and legends about ancient heroes. He also read a series of novels about a naval captain named Horatio Hornblower. Perhaps it was these tales of adventure on the high seas that encouraged his love of sailing.

Ted also wrote poetry as a teenager. Much of it was about war and conquest. Young Ted's other interests included hunting and taxidermy, the art of stuffing fish, birds, and other dead animals.

Learning the Value of Money

Ed Turner also wanted Ted to learn the value of money and how to set financial goals for himself. For this reason, Ted was assigned to do a heavy load of chores at home in order to earn his allowance. And by the time he was in his late teens, his father charged him rent during the summer vacations he spent at home.

Ted even had to help pay for his own high-school graduation present. When Ted graduated from McCallie, his father offered to give him part of the money to buy a small sailboat if Ted could come up with the rest. Ted's share of the cost of the boat ate up all of his savings.

THE IMPORTANCE OF SUCCESS

Ed Turner's most significant contribution to his son's life was probably the way he constantly talked about the importance of success. Even when Ted was quite young, his father would often sit him down for serious discussions about Ted's future, about what Ted needed to do in order to be a winner.

Ted Turner grew up to become a very competitive man, with a strong drive to win at everything he tried. He admits that the seeds of his high ambition were planted during his childhood.

"My father had this burning desire to succeed," Ted says. "Success, success, success! And I went to this military school where they pounded in, 'You got to get to the top, boy, you got to get to the top.' Well, I got to the top."

Chapter 4

A Young Rebel

Because of his strong interest in sailing and the military, Ted wanted to attend the United States Naval Academy after graduating from McCallie. But Ed Turner would not hear of it. His own plans for his son's future called for Ted to attend one of the highly respected East Coast universities that are called the Ivy League schools.

Ted tried to get into Harvard University, in Cambridge, Massachusetts, a school that some people think is the best in the United States. But Harvard did not accept his application. He ended up instead going to Brown University in Providence, Rhode Island.

COLLEGE DAYS

Ted's competitive spirit was strong at Brown. During his first year at college, he entered a number of sailboat races in which crews from different colleges competed. He won every one of them.

FAMILY TRAGEDIES

Ted's teenage years were filled with discipline at home and rebellion at school. Meanwhile, his younger sister, Mary Jane, was suffering from a terrible illness. When she was twelve and Ted was fifteen, she was stricken with lupus erythematosus, a particularly serious disease in which the body's systems slowly go bad. It is a disease that cannot be cured, and it causes a great deal of pain. After five years of illness, Mary Jane died at the age of seventeen.

Around the same time, Ted's mother, Florence Turner, and his father were divorced. Now that he was alone with his father, Ted felt more pressure than ever to succeed, to be a good son, and to win his father's respect.

Learning About Business

Ed Turner endlessly lectured to his son about business and economics. Ted remembers that as the two drove to work together, his father would talk about tax laws, sales, management, construction, and a host of other topics. "He told me how he got started, what happened in competitive situations, how he lost business and how he got it," remembers Ted.

The young man listened and learned, and his business career seemed to start off well. In the fall of 1960, close to his twenty-second birthday, Ted was made the general manager of the Macon, Georgia, branch of Turner Advertising Company.

Two years later, Ed Turner bought a bigger company in Atlanta. The Atlanta company was now the largest section of the Turner business, and Ed Turner promised Ted that it would someday belong to him. But beneath the surface, things were not going well at Turner Advertising Company. Ed Turner was having problems.

Ted's father had achieved the success that he had sought so eagerly. He had made millions of dollars. But he had also begun suffering from spells of deep depression, during which it was hard for him to concentrate on running the business. He had borrowed money to buy the Atlanta company, and now the Turner business was nearly $6 million in debt. Ed Turner became convinced that he had made a mistake in buying the Atlanta company, and he decided to sell it.

A CRISIS

When Ted learned of his father's plans to sell the Atlanta company, he was surprised and angry. He could not understand how his father, who had always encouraged him to be a fighter and to move boldly ahead in life, could be thinking about selling out. To Ted, it seemed as though his father were giving up—something he had taught Ted never to do.

Ted confronted Ed Turner and the two had an argument. Ted repeated all the warnings against being a quitter that he had heard from his father over the years. Tragically, however, Ed Turner was in the grip of serious depression, which Ted Turner later described as "a nervous breakdown."

Ed Turner's condition worsened. On March 5, 1963, he went into the study of his plantation-style mansion and killed himself with a pistol. Ed Turner was fifty-three years old at the time of his death; Ted was twenty-four. On top of the grief and shock that Ted felt at his father's death, he now faced his first major business challenge. Could he keep Turner Advertising alive?

Chapter 5

On the Frontier of Television

After his father's death, Ted Turner discovered that Turner Advertising was worth about $1 million. But it had debts that totaled many times that amount. This was bad enough, but there was another unexpected turn of events in store for Turner as well.

Before he died, Ed Turner had signed an agreement to sell his company. Now the buyers expected the sale to go through as planned. But Ted turned the tables and surprised everyone.

Turner decided to keep the company even after his financial advisors told him that it was a bad idea. But although he was only twenty-four years old, Ted was quite capable of making up his own mind and then sticking firmly to his decision, something that he has continued to do throughout his career. He stubbornly insisted that he would somehow manage to keep the company. He also vowed to build it into a success and restore the fortunes of Turner Advertising.

A BIG CHALLENGE

Turner's first task was to get the sale of the Atlanta company cancelled. To do this, he had to persuade the buyers to change their minds. He resorted to all sorts of tricks to make the company seem less desirable to the buyers. For one thing, he transferred the company's top employees, whose skills and knowledge would be valuable to the new owners, away from Atlanta to the Macon, Georgia, branch of the business. He also told the buyers that if they insisted on the sale going through, he would find a way to put his own billboards up "right in front of theirs."

This no-holds-barred attack worked. The buyers agreed to cancel the agreement of sale in return for a payment from Turner of $200,000. He was delighted; he could keep the company. There was just one hitch—he didn't have the $200,000.

Making a Deal

At this point, Turner displayed the gambler's instinct that has guided him through many business deals. He knew that if he made the $200,000 payment to the buyers right away, as their arrangement called for, most of the money would go for taxes. (The buyers had not owned the company long enough to qualify for the maximum tax deduction on the money they made when they sold the company back to Turner.) So he took a chance and delayed the payment until he had time to raise the money.

Ted guessed the buyers would be willing to accept a late payment so their taxes would be lower. His guess was correct, and the deal was made. Many acquaintances think that getting back his father's company was the biggest challenge Turner has ever faced. Now he would discover whether he could run the company.

NEW VENTURES

Turner proved to be a better businessman than his father, and the company soon became very profitable. Over the next few years, Turner was able to buy other billboard companies. He also began acquiring radio stations.

One secret of Turner's success is that he does not believe in letting valuable resources go to waste. He is good at finding ways to make use of things. So when he started out in the radio business, he put up posters advertising his radio stations on any of the Turner Advertising billboards that were not already rented out.

Raising a Family

While he was becoming established as a businessman, Turner was also becoming a family man. He met and married a woman named Judy Nye. The couple had two children, Laura Lee Turner and Robert Edward Turner, IV. Both were born in the early 1960s.

In 1964, after his marriage to Judy Nye had ended in divorce, Turner married for a second time. His new bride was Janie Shirley Smith, a former airline stewardess from Birmingham, Alabama. Ted and Janie had three children: Rhett (who was named for Rhett Butler, the famous character played by actor Clark Gable in Turner's favorite movie, *Gone with the Wind*), Beauregard, and Jennie.

The two children from Turner's first marriage also made their home with Ted and Janie. So, by the end of the 1960s, the Turner household had five children in all. Ted and Janie were divorced in 1988. In the fall of 1990, Turner announced plans to marry actress Jane Fonda.

Ted Turner and Janie, his second wife, with his five children in 1976. (©1991 Jay/Leviton-Atlanta.)

Turner and his son Rhett in their South Carolina home. Rhett, who was 16 when this picture was taken, was named after the hero of Gone with the Wind. (©1991 David Burnett/Contact Press Images.)

Captain Outrageous

During the 1960s and 1970s, Turner was often away from home for months at a time. He had long been an expert small-boat sailor, and now he discovered a more challenging aspect of sailing: world-class deep-water racing. His business was running smoothly and profitably, so he was able to spend the time and money needed to become involved in ocean racing.

Ted Turner soon began making a name for himself in the yachting and racing world. He won several important races, including the very difficult Southern Ocean Racing Circuit in 1966 and again in 1970.

In 1974, Turner competed in what is generally thought to be the world's most famous sailboat race, the America's Cup. He did not win the America's Cup that year, but he received a lot of attention from the news media.

Most yachtsmen appear stuffy and reserved, but Turner came across as rowdy and colorful. He would swear fiercely at his crew one moment and then joke with them the next. He was outspoken and energetic, like a wild breeze of fresh air in the tight-knit, somewhat snobbish yachting community. The press started calling him "Captain Outrageous."

GETTING INTO TELEVISION

Meanwhile, a turning point in Turner's life had occurred in 1970. That year he bought Channel 17, a small, rundown television station in Atlanta. The station was not a money-maker. In fact, at the time Turner became interested in it, it was losing more than $500,000 each year.

Once again, Turner's financial advisors warned him against the move. They told him that the station couldn't possibly make money. They also reminded him that he didn't know anything about the TV business.

But once again, Ted Turner followed his instinct and went ahead anyway. He later explained, "I just love it when people say I can't do something. There's nothing that makes me feel better, because all my life people have said I wasn't going to make it."

Turner also said, "The secret of my success is this: Every time, I tried to go as far as I could. When I climbed the hills, I saw the mountains. Then I started climbing the mountains." When he succeeded with billboards, he tried radio. When he succeeded with radio, he decided it was time to try television.

Going Public

Turner Advertising had always been a privately owned company—owned by the Turner family. But now, in order to raise money to buy Channel 17, Turner had to take his company public. In other words, he had to form a corporation and sell shares of **stock.** He kept enough of the shares, however, to give him control of the company, although he was no longer the sole owner.

Public Corporations

To finance his expansion into television, Ted Turner took his company public. This means that he turned what had once been a privately owned company into a publicly owned corporation. Anyone could buy part of this corporation.

> The pieces of a public corporation that are sold to the general public are called shares of stock. Each share of stock represents a very small part of the total ownership of a corporation. When someone invests in a company by buying shares of stock, that person—called a stockholder or shareholder—owns those shares of the company.
>
> In many cases, when a private company goes public, its owners sell fewer than half of the shares and keep more than half of the shares for themselves. This gives them control of the company. In such cases, they are called the majority stockholders.
>
> Ted Turner retained the majority of shares in his company when he turned it into a public corporation. In this way, he raised funds by selling stock but he did not give up control of the company.

Channel 17 was a **UHF** station. That is, it was an independent station that was not affiliated with, or connected to, one of the major networks. Unlike **VHF** stations, most of which broadcast the shows provided by the three major networks, UHF stations must provide their own programming. They usually show a lot of reruns of old TV series and a lot of local sports events. This is what Turner had in mind for Channel 17, and also for another station that he bought in Charlotte, North Carolina.

A Flair for Showmanship

Atlanta had five television stations, with Channel 17 at the bottom of the heap. But Turner quickly demonstrated a flair for showmanship. He tried all sorts of stunts to call attention to Channel 17.

For example, when one of the big-three networks decided not to use several shows, Turner bought the right to broadcast these rejects. He then put up billboards all over town saying, "NBC Is Moving to Channel 17."

And when the owners of a rival UHF station closed that station down, Turner celebrated the event with an on-the-air "Thank You, Atlanta" party featuring bands and balloons. He acted as though Channel 17 had beaten the other station, even though the other station had been more popular right up until the end.

These incidents illustrate a key ingredient in Ted Turner's success story: he has the gift of creating excitement.

Channel 17 lost $500,000 dollars in 1970 and again in 1971. But by 1972 the station was making money, and in 1973 it earned more than a million dollars. Ted Turner had turned it around. Before long, Turner's Atlanta and Charlotte stations were two of the most successful independent TV stations in the country.

Programming Strategy

Turner's programming strategy was simple. He broadcast the Atlanta Braves baseball games, the Atlanta Hawks basketball games, professional wrestling shows, and a mixture of old situation comedies such as *Gilligan's Island* and *Leave It to Beaver.*

One thing that Channel 17 didn't offer much of was news. At 6 P.M., when the VHF stations showed the evening news, Channel 17 showed *Star Trek*. In fact, Turner's stations broadcast only the minimum amount of news required by the Federal Communications Commission (FCC), which was forty minutes each day.

On Turner's stations, the news appeared in the early morning hours. He was convinced that his viewers wanted entertainment and did not want to be bothered with the news. Later, when he decided to start CNN, this attitude would make it difficult for him to convince people that he was serious about creating an all-news station.

Chapter 6

The Cable Revolution

The nature of television changed during the early 1970s, as advances were made in cable technology. At first, cable TV was simply a way for outlying rural areas to have better television reception. From antennas that were put up on mountaintops, cables were run down into television sets in homes in the valleys. Soon cable companies were formed around the country. With their special antennas, they would pick up big-city TV stations and, for a fee, pipe them into homes by cable.

JOINING THE CABLE REVOLUTION

Turner was one of the first TV station owners to see the possibilities of cable. He started sending his Atlanta station's signal to cable companies in other parts of the South by **microwave.**

Audiences in rural areas loved cable TV, because they could now watch professional sports events. And the advantage for Turner was that the larger his viewing audience became, the more money he could charge companies that advertised on his station.

A new era in cable started in 1975, when Radio Corporation of America (RCA) launched a space satellite called Satcom I, which was positioned above the United States. The satellite carried transponders, which are devices that picked up television signals from stations on earth and rebroadcast them over the whole country.

Broadcasters could lease transponders from RCA and use them to send their signal to cable-company operators across the entire nation. The first broadcaster to do so was Home Box Office (HBO), which started beaming movies to cable subscribers in 1975. The second was Ted Turner.

THE SUPERSTATION

Turner had the imagination and vision to see that Satcom I was a new frontier in television. He wanted to be one of the first pioneers to explore this frontier. The week after HBO began broadcasting its signal from space, he flew to New York to start making arrangements to lease a transponder.

Turner leased one transponder, at a cost of about a million dollars a year, and spent another $750,000 building an earth station to transmit his signal up to the satellite. Then, in December of 1976, he began broadcasting Channel 17 to cable operators nationwide. He renamed the station WTBS (the letters stand for Turner Broadcasting System), and he called it "the SuperStation that serves the nation."

Buying Sports Teams

One of the things that had made Channel 17 successful on cable was broadcasting the Atlanta Braves baseball games and the Atlanta Hawks basketball games. Turner knew that the teams would be essential to the success of WTBS as well. But he was afraid that the team owners would start charging him a lot more for the right to broadcast the games once the station went nationwide. He was also afraid that the teams might move to another city.

Because he couldn't risk losing them, Turner simply bought the Braves in 1976. Now that he was the owner of the team, he could be certain that they wouldn't move! The following year, he bought a controlling interest, or majority share, of the Hawks.

THE MOUTH OF THE SOUTH

The first years of WTBS were busy and exciting ones for Ted Turner. When the station went on the air, some critics said, "Why should people around the country want to watch Turner's dinky little UHF station and his old reruns?" But the critics were wrong. WTBS became popular.

Audiences liked WTBS because it offered an alternative to the major networks. Its mixture of sports and light-hearted comedies appealed to many Americans, especially those in rural areas.

During the late 1970s, WTBS attracted national advertisers and became very profitable, earning millions of dollars each year. (It is still the most profitable part of Ted Turner's broadcasting empire.) And while he was building his SuperStation, Turner himself was also becoming a national celebrity.

In 1977, Turner won the America's cup, the most famous sailing race in the world, in his yacht Courageous. *Other yachtsmen called him Captain Outrageous.* (Anestis Diakopoulos.)

Winning the America's Cup

Part of Turner's fame had to do with sailing. In 1977, as captain of his yacht *Courageous,* he won the America's Cup, the most famous prize in sailing.

Cigar-chomping, loud-talking Turner was a very lively winner. The press went wild, providing him with a wealth of free publicity. He even appeared on the cover of *Sports Illustrated* and in many other magazines. In short, he lived up to the nickname Captain Outrageous.

After Turner bought the Atlanta Braves baseball team in 1976, more people started coming to the games. Some of them came just to watch Turner's antics. (Michael Keza/Gamma Liaison.)

The Boss of the Braves

Turner gained a new nickname around this time. People started calling him the "Mouth of the South," largely because of some well-publicized arguments he had with Bowie Kuhn, the commissioner of baseball.

One day, disgusted by the Braves' poor performance, Turner went into his team's locker room, put on a uniform, and took over the job of manager of the team. Because such action was against the rules of the league, Kuhn penalized Turner. The two men had many shouting matches and confrontations that made headline news, and also made people more curious than ever about Ted Turner.

The Braves were not a very good team, and they lost more games than they won. But Turner wanted fans to come to the ballpark to watch his team, so he started pulling stunts to attract attention.

Before one game, Turner climbed onto an ostrich and galloped wildly around the infield on it, astonishing the fans. Another time, he challenged Tug McGraw, a star pitcher for the Philadelphia Phillies, to a baseball-rolling contest. The two were supposed to roll baseballs to home base with their noses.

Ted Turner is nothing if not competitive. Even in the trivial contest with McGraw, he went all out to win. Recalls one executive from the Braves, "Tug was just gently pushing the ball along, while Ted was getting his nose absolutely bloody. There was no skin left on the end of it. Needless to say, he won."

Turner soon developed a loyal following in Atlanta and throughout the South. The fans loved his stunts and shows. Many of them admitted that they came to the games not to see the Braves but to see what antics Ted Turner would be up to next. But even while he was clowning for the fans and the cameras, Turner was getting ready for his next big step in broadcasting.

Chapter 7

Launching CNN

Ted Turner likes to claim that he always thinks and plans several moves ahead. While he was still launching WTBS, he had already begun to think about an all-news cable network. And by the time WTBS was beginning to prove itself, Turner had already moved on to his next project—CNN.

EARNING RESPECT

Getting CNN started was not easy. First of all, people in the news business knew that Turner had not shown much respect for TV news. However, Turner solved this problem by hiring one of the most respected newsmen in the country as the first president of CNN. This was Reese Schonfeld, who had been involved in TV news for 25 years.

Schonfeld knew everyone in the TV news business. Soon he

was hiring many talented editors, reporters, and newscasters away from the networks, bringing them to Atlanta to work for CNN. A number of former network stars, such as anchorman Daniel Schorr, switched to CNN.

MEETING CHALLENGES

In May of 1979, Ted Turner announced boldly that CNN would begin broadcasting in June of 1980. That gave Schonfeld and his team just one year to start a completely new television enterprise from scratch. There were many problems to solve and many decisions to make.

For one thing, Schonfeld and Turner had to sell advertisers and cable companies on the idea that viewers would *watch* CNN, especially for live news. Schonfeld explained over and over again that CNN would cover as many live stories as possible. "Aren't you going to wind up covering a lot of little, two-alarm fires that don't amount to anything?" he was once asked.

"I'm afraid so," Schonfeld answered, "but until the fire is over, you don't know whether it's a two-alarmer or the fire that burned down Chicago!" He added that CNN wouldn't dare leave the story until they knew for sure how it ended—and neither would the viewers.

The Fastnet Disaster

One key to Turner's and Schonfeld's vision of a live, as-it-happens news show was an "open" newsroom. This would be a room in which the anchors would be surrounded by producers, cameramen,

In the shadow of expensive satellite equipment, staff members take a lunch break at CNN's Atlanta headquarters. One secret of Turner's success was luring talented people to CNN from the big-three networks. (Alan S. Weiner/NYT Pictures.)

editors, and all their equipment. This would give viewers a look at how news gets on the air, and it would make CNN seem closer to reality than the slickly packaged network news shows.

A station in Vancouver, Canada, was using a similar type of newsroom. So Schonfeld flew to Vancouver with Bunky Helfrich, the architect who was building the CNN studio, to show him what he had in mind.

At the same time, Turner was away on one of his frequent sailing absences. In his 61-foot yacht *Tenacious,* he was competing in the Fastnet Race off the coast of Ireland.

While Schonfeld and Helfrich were flying north to Vancouver, Turner and his crew, along with the other boats competing in the Fastnet, were sailing into a huge storm at sea. Winds screamed by at more than seventy miles per hour, and the boats were buffeted by twenty-five-foot waves. Sailboats started capsizing. The 1979 Fastnet turned into the worst disaster in the history of yachting.

Survival at Sea

All this was unknown to Schonfeld and Helfrich as they walked into the TV studio in Vancouver. Seeing them, a producer said, "Why are you guys here?"

"What do you mean?" Schonfeld asked, bewildered.

"Don't you know? Your boss is missing."

"Missing?"

"They think he's dead."

Numb with shock, Schonfeld and Helfrich watched the news from Plymouth, England. They learned that rescue helicopters had failed to spot the *Tenacious* along the storm-tossed course of the race. Suddenly, to their relief and amazement, there on the monitor was Ted Turner, weary but alive.

Although fifteen yachtsmen had died in the storm, Turner had survived because he had forced his crew to keep sailing at full speed into the wind—in fact, to keep *racing*—throughout the entire storm. He not only survived, he also won the race.

The helicopters failed to find Turner because he had already gone past them. Perhaps that race was the best example of what has made Ted Turner so successful—the ability to keep moving ahead on course no matter how bad things get.

Satellite Troubles

After his brush with death, Turner continued with preparations to launch CNN. But disaster threatened again in December of 1979, when RCA's Satcom III satellite was launched. Turner had arranged to broadcast CNN from a transponder aboard Satcom III. Unfortunately, the satellite vanished from radar screens after three days in space and was given up for lost. With less than six months to go before the scheduled start of broadcasting, suddenly CNN found itself without a transponder. Everyone at CNN headquarters thought the situation was hopeless. But Turner sent word for them to "Carry on!" Somehow, they would find a way.

At this point, the entire future of CNN was at stake. If the network failed to start up on the scheduled date, advertisers and cable companies would lose faith, and Ted Turner's reputation would suffer a serious blow. The station might never recover; the whole plan for CNN might have to be scrapped.

Risking everything on one bold move, Turner sued RCA, demanding that the company give him a transponder on one of its other satellites. He won a court order giving him the use of a Satcom I transponder, and then RCA replaced the lost Satcom III with a new satellite.

Signing Up Cable Companies

Another challenge faced by Turner in the months before CNN started broadcasting was winning the support of cable companies. He needed them to subscribe to his service so that he could guarantee viewers to the companies that advertised on the network. CNN's survival depended upon advertising and upon the subscriber fees paid by the cable industry.

However, many cable-system operators were doubtful about an all-news station. Turner tried to stir up their feelings of loyalty by reminding them how much Channel 17, and later WTBS, had done for the cable industry. He also reminded them that he had believed in the future of cable from the start. To the tune of a popular country-and-western song, he sang, "I Was Cable When Cable Wasn't Cool," dressed up like a cowboy and toting a guitar.

RAPID GROWTH

Despite Turner's promotional antics, the cable industry was slow to jump on the CNN bandwagon. Many operators decided to "wait and see" before signing up. So when the station came on the air in June of 1980, it reached only 1.7 million homes.

By the end of 1980, however, 663 new cable systems had subscribed to CNN, and the station was reaching 4.3 million homes. The number continued to rise. By the fall of 1990, CNN was reaching 56.5 million homes in more than ninety countries.

Chapter 8

Making History

From the time of its successful launch in June 1980, when it scooped the major networks by interviewing President Carter in Fort Wayne, CNN has changed the course of television news. There were mishaps, of course, especially in the early days, when the crew was new and inexperienced.

Once anchorman Dan Schorr's clothes caught on fire on the air when a lightbulb exploded. On another occasion, anchorman Bernie Shaw was delivering the news from his desk on the set. Suddenly, a cleaning woman, not realizing that she was on camera, walked in, picked up Shaw's wastepaper basket, dumped it into a bin, and moved on. Shaw just kept talking, trying to keep a straight face. For the most part, however, viewers forgave these occasional glitches, because the show delivered sound, detailed, and reliable news coverage.

SEBASTIAN MIDDLE SCHOOL
MEDIA CENTER
KY 41339

MAJOR ACHIEVEMENTS

In its first few years on the air, CNN scored some remarkable victories. In 1981, it broadcast the most complete footage of the release of American hostages from Iran. It also was the first to report that President Ronald Reagan had been wounded in an assassination attempt in Washington, D.C.

CNN received high praise for its coverage of the Democratic and Republican presidential conventions and the elections of 1980, 1984, and 1988. And it won the George Foster Peabody Award for its live, worldwide coverage of the stock market crash in 1987.

Drama in China

Perhaps the most dramatic event in CNN's history occurred in May of 1989, when thousands of students and others in Beijing, China, rallied to call for democratic reforms to their strict communist government. Nothing like this had ever happened in China, and CNN was there to provide coverage.

The news team had brought in a portable satellite dish and kept broadcasting, even though word came from the Chinese government that the broadcast might be shut down at any moment. On May 20, CNN's viewers around the world watched a tense scene in the Beijing hotel room that served as CNN headquarters. A stern-faced Chinese official ordered the live coverage to stop. With visible reluctance, the news team signed off.

A California newspaper reported that this scene "was a historic piece of television, providing the most graphic illustration imaginable of a repressive government in action. . . . For CNN, the disappearing coverage was a coup for the ages. Nothing in recent TV history could equal it. For pure live drama, it's difficult to imagine that anything will ever surpass it."

Suing the President

CNN won many victories, but it often had to fight for them. Turner had to sue the big-three networks, President Ronald Reagan, and several high-ranking members of Reagan's administration. He claimed that the long-standing arrangement by which the White House shared information with CBS, NBC, and ABC was a violation of CNN's right to take part in news-sharing.

The White House eventually agreed to include CNN in all news-sharing activities, and the lawsuit was settled out of court. From that time on, CNN was accepted on an equal footing with the other networks. The President even had a special TV set installed in his office so that he could watch CNN. So did other prominent figures, including Prime Minister Margaret Thatcher of Great Britain.

The networks responded to Turner's success by increasing the competition. They began showing more news. ABC even launched a rival satellite news channel called Satellite News Channel (SNC), but Ted Turner bought SNC in 1983 and closed it down. Although CNN's budget was only a fraction of what the big networks could spend on news, CNN managed to hold its own and eventually to win respect.

The Gulf War

CNN made history once again in 1990–91, during the Persian Gulf War. This war pitted the United States, Saudi Arabia, Great Britain, and more than a dozen other allies against the Middle Eastern nation of Iraq, which had invaded the small country of Kuwait on the Persian Gulf.

For many weeks, CNN provided round-the-clock coverage of the war: first the events leading up to the war, and then the war itself. World leaders and generals, as well as millions of ordinary citizens, stayed tuned to CNN to see what was happening on the battlefront.

Early in the war, Iraq's president, Saddam Hussein, declared that his government would censor (review and approve) every news broadcast from Iraq. At this, most foreign journalists left the country. But CNN's Peter Arnett stayed in Baghdad, the capital of Iraq, and continued to issue reports, although the Iraqi government would not allow him to say anything it did not agree with.

Some Americans felt that CNN should have left Iraq rather than submit to censorship by the enemy. But others felt that CNN's broadcasts from Iraq provided a valuable service during the war, even though Arnett could not speak freely. Once again, CNN had stirred up debate by doing what no other station dared to do.

BEYOND CNN

Ted Turner never simply sits still and enjoys success. The completion of one venture is the time to start something else. Since launching CNN, he has continued to develop his broadcasting empire.

In 1982, he started a second cable news channel. It was called CNN2, or Headline News, and it consisted of short newscasts updated every half-hour around the clock. That same year, he founded a twenty-four-hour, all-news radio show called CNN Radio. He also made a deal with the Cousteau Society to produce original TV programs about the explorations of the famous scuba diver and marine scientist, Jacques Cousteau.

The SuperStation, WTBS, continued to be the centerpiece of Turner Broadcasting. During the 1980s, it began adding original programs to its mix of reruns and sports. Many of these original programs were based on Ted Turner's own ideas. One was a fifty-five-part series called "Portrait of America," which won a Peabody Award in 1984. Another was a movie called *Threads*, which showed the aftereffects of a nuclear war. It premiered on WTBS in 1985 and was the most-watched program in the history of cable TV.

The Purchase of MGM

One of Turner's most controversial ventures occurred in 1986, when he spent $1.6 billion to purchase the MGM Entertainment Company. He had to go deeply into debt to finance this deal, and many people criticized him for making it. But Turner claimed that it was his most spectacular business deal yet.

In exchange for his $1.6 billion, Turner became the owner of MGM's film studio, television production company, video distribution business, and Hollywood real estate. But the biggest prize of all was MGM's film library, a collection of more than 3,000 movies to which MGM owned the **copyrights.** This library included such classic films as *Casablanca, Singin' in the Rain, The Wizard of Oz, 2001: A Space Odyssey,* and Turner's own favorite, *Gone with the Wind.*

Within just a few months, Turner had resold all parts of MGM except the film library. He used the profits from selling the other businesses to help pay the interest on the money he had borrowed to buy MGM in the first place. He kept only the film library, which is what he had wanted all along. The movies were used to attract viewers to his TV stations and as the basis of a video distribution company.

In 1988, Turner launched yet another cable station, TNT (for Turner Network Television). Its first broadcast was *Gone with the Wind*, which was shown on television for the first time ever. The movie was seen in 17 million homes. "The Making of a Legend," an original program about the movie's history, won a Peabody Award for TNT the following year. It gave Ted Turner great satisfaction to own the movie that had always been his favorite—and it gave him even more satisfaction to share it with the nation on his own TV station.

Chapter 9

Lead, Follow, or Get Out of the Way

Ted Turner says that his philosophy of life has changed over the years. As a young man, he was driven by the need to achieve personal success, to become rich and powerful. Much of this need was instilled in him by his ambitious father. But after his father's death, Ted Turner struggled for a long time trying to figure out just what "success" really is.

Throughout his career, Turner has kept a photograph of his father in his office. But he has also learned to think for himself about what success really means to him. He once said about his father, "I loved that man desperately; we were very close; but I spent a lot of time trying to figure out what it was that he did wrong. He put too much emphasis on material success [money and possessions]. I can tell you it's fool's gold."

ENJOYING LIFE'S PLEASURES

Ted Turner has always enjoyed the pleasures that money can bring. Yachting, for example, is a rich person's sport. And he likes owning large plantations and ranches, such as his 131,000-acre spread in Montana.

But Turner also has always had a penny-pinching streak as well. He drives a modest American-made car instead of an expensive imported one. And for years, gossip columnists loved to point out that he shined his own shoes and had his wife cut his hair to save money.

DOING GOOD

Turner now claims to enjoy making money not for the sake of the money itself, but because of what he can do with it: spread information, improve people's understanding of one another, and possibly help enlighten the world. He frequently speaks out on such issues as environmental protection, human rights, and the antiwar movement. The real value of riches, he says, is that they enable you to do more good in the world.

Turner sums up his global philosophy this way: "You've got to basically believe that human beings, when confronted with the information, will choose the intelligent course. . . . With the right information, we hopefully are going to make the right decisions."

The Goodwill Games

One way Turner has put his philosophy into action is by sponsoring the Goodwill Games. This is an international athletic event that Turner organized with officials in the Soviet Union. The first Good-

At the first Goodwill Games, held in Moscow in 1976, Turner awards a medal to a winning athlete. Turner believes that friendly competition can help bring nations closer together. (Jasmin/Gamma Liaison.)

will Games were held in Moscow in 1986 and involved athletes from sixty countries; the second took place in Seattle, Washington, in 1990.

Turner plans to continue sponsoring the Goodwill Games in 1994 and 1998. He believes that international communication and cooperation—including some *friendly* competition—are the keys to avoiding nuclear war.

Sailing trophies and journalism awards fill the shelves in Ted Turner's Atlanta office. (Alan S. Weiner/NYT Pictures.)

A MAN WITH DRIVE

Ted Turner's office in the CNN Center in downtown Atlanta is full of mementos of his eventful career: dozens of sailing trophies, some journalism awards, stuffed fish and ducks. But on the desk are two objects that seem to sum up Turner's special blend of courage, leadership, and gambling instinct.

One of these objects is a pair of dice made of crystal, from the famous jewelry store Tiffany's. Perhaps for Turner these dice represent not only the riches he has achieved but the many risks he has taken along the way.

The other object is a plaque with Turner's favorite motto: "Lead, Follow, or Get Out of the Way." He has little use for anyone who simply drifts through life with no purpose or drive. And whatever else can be said about Ted Turner, no one will ever accuse him of lacking drive.

Glossary

anchor (or anchorperson)   The person who delivers television news; usually two or three anchors work at one time.

bureau   An office maintained by a network at some location far from network headquarters.

cable television   Television broadcasts that enter viewers' sets through a wire (cable), not over the airwaves.

copyright   The right of ownership in a creative work, such as a book, song, or movie.

corporation   A group of people formed to carry on a business enterprise, with legally given rights and duties.

entrepreneur   A person who organizes, manages, and takes all the risk of running a business.

Great Depression   A period during the 1930s of low economic activity in the United States, with much unemployment.

microwave   A special type of electric wave that is used in radar and to send television signals over long distances.

network   A large company that produces shows and news broadcasts for nationwide distribution by radio or television.

stock   A certificate of ownership in a company.

UHF   Abbreviation for "ultrahigh frequency," a frequency range in which some television stations broadcast their signals. UHF stations have higher station numbers than VHF stations. (See VHF.)

VHF   Abbreviation for "very high frequency," a frequency range in which some television stations broadcast their signals.

yachtsman   Someone who sails large boats (yachts) for racing or pleasure cruising.

Index

SEBASTIAN MIDDLE SCHOOL
MEDIA CENTER
JACKSON, KY 41339